Looking after my pet

Goldfish

DAVID ALDERTON

LORENZ BOOKS

Introduction

Whether you live in an apartment or a house, a goldfish is a great choice as a pet. Goldfish are easy to take care of, and they can become very tame, taking food out of your fingers. There's also a wide variety of shapes and colors to choose from, and these fish can often live for 10 years or more. The oldest known goldfish on record was over 40 years old when she died.

Goldfish are easy pets to look after, and they can live for a very long time if they are taken care of properly.

Pond life

Some types of goldfish can be kept in a garden pond throughout the year, although if the weather is likely to become very cold in the winter and the pond is likely to freeze, then you may have to move your fish. It is, of course, much more expensive to build a pond for goldfish, compared to keeping them in a tank indoors, and it also requires much more space.

You can keep goldfish in a pond outside, where they will live happily in a group, but you may have to protect them from cats and birds such as herons and seagulls.

Keeping your goldfish in a tank indoors is easier than building a pond. However, a tank does need to be kept clean. It can have some gravel, oxygenating plants, and ornaments to make it look nice, and a cover to stop the fish from jumping out.

Popular pets

Goldfish originally come from southern China, where they have been bred for over 1,000 years. The people there used to catch fish known as carp in rivers. Most carp were a dull, green color, but people found that a few had orange areas on their bodies. They kept these and bred from them, and so started to create the many goldfish varieties that exist today. Goldfish were first taken from China to Japan in about 1500, and then on the long journey to Europe about 200 years later. Goldfish are now the most common household pet in the world.

Goldfish are descended from carp, which are still found in rivers. This ornamental carp, known as Koi, is a close relative of the goldfish but much larger.

Looking after goldfish

Although goldfish do not need to be groomed and walked like a dog, they still require daily care. They should normally be fed every day, and their aquarium should be cleaned on a regular basis, with some of the old water being taken out and replaced with fresh water.

Goldfish that live in a pond also need to be fed, and you must keep the water level here topped up, too, especially when the weather is warm. If the fish are living outdoors during the winter, you do need to make sure that ice is not allowed to cover the entire surface of the water.

Goldfish do not take up as much of your time as a pet cat or dog would, but their aquarium still needs to be kept very clean and the fish need to be fed daily.

What is a goldfish?

Goldfish rely on their fins to help them move. The number of fins that goldfish have differs, depending on the variety. Ordinary common goldfish have seven fins, but other varieties bred from the common goldfish, known as fancy goldfish, may have a different number of fins. One type of fancy goldfish, called lionheads, have no dorsal fin on the top of their body, making them poor swimmers.

This lionhead goldfish is unusual in that it does not have a dorsal fin on the top of its body.

The long, slim body of the comet goldfish makes it a good swimmer and ideal for keeping in a pond.

Strong swimmers

Some goldfish, such as the comet, are more powerful swimmers than others. You can easily recognize these by their long, slim shape, and a powerful tail fin that allows them to move through the water quickly. These goldfish are well suited to living in ponds, whereas fancy goldfish have a more rounded body shape, which prevents them from swimming so fast.

Breathing underwater

Goldfish do not need to come up to the surface of the water to breathe. In fact, if they do, this is a sign that something is wrong. They usually rely on their gills to take oxygen out of the water. If you look behind the goldfish's eyes on each side of the head, there is a C-shaped area that forms the gill cover. As the covers move, water passes over the gills, which are hidden out of sight. Oxygen then travels through the gills into the bloodstream.

Goldfish breathe by taking oxygen out of the water.

Swim bladder

Air is trapped in an organ called the swim bladder. This organ is important as it allows the fish to control the depth at which they swim. Sometimes, when a fish is sick, the swim bladder may not function properly, causing the fish to lie at an angle or float near the surface.

Body defense

If you look closely at a goldfish, you will see that its body is covered in overlapping scales. These help to protect it from sickness. When you catch a goldfish, be extremely careful not to damage the scales, since any break or scratch can allow an infection to develop.

The scales on a goldfish are made from a hard, bony substance. An infection may develop if there is any damage caused to the scales.

No stomach

Unlike humans, goldfish do not have a stomach where they can store food. Instead, they eat small amounts of food regularly during the day so they do not become hungry.

Goldfish will use their jaws to dig in the gravel in search of food. They naturally eat plants and small water creatures.

The senses

When it comes to finding their way around in the water, goldfish can use their eyes, but they also get information from their lateral line. You may be able to locate this slightly lighter area that runs down each side of the body, in the shape of a narrow line. This part of the fish's body is full of nerves, which pick up movements in the water nearby, and so can alert the goldfish to possible danger.

fins

lateral line

eyes

scales

gills

Different types of goldfish

No one knows the exact number of goldfish varieties that exist today, but there are certainly well over a hundred. Many of these, such as the pearlscale, were first bred in China. In spite of their name, not all goldfish are a golden-orange color. There are white, chocolate, blue, and black goldfish, as well as multicolored and speckled varieties.

Goldfish come in many colors. You might like to get a white or black fish to make your aquarium look more exciting.

Common goldfish

These were the first goldfish. They are still very popular and may be kept both indoors and outdoors in ponds. They will get much bigger in ponds, and may reach a size of 12 inches or more. The color of common goldfish can vary from shades of yellow to red.

Shubunkins are slender and they have individual, multicolored patterns.

Shubunkin

You can recognize shubunkins by their sleek shape and multicolored patterns. They may differ widely in color, and some are much darker than others. Their patterns are very individual, and can include white, orange, blue, violet, and black markings. If you want shubunkins for a pond, it is better to choose bright-colored ones, since you will be able to locate them more easily in the dark water.

Lionhead and oranda

As they get older, these fish develop a raspberrylike swelling over their head, known as a hood. They are bred in a large variety of colors, and are usually housed in aquariums, although they must not be kept too warm.

Orandas have a distinctive, raspberrylike swelling over their head. Lionheads are similar, but have no dorsal fin on the top of their body.

6

The white marks on its scales look like pearls, so giving the pearlscale its name.

Pearlscale

These goldfish have white areas on their scales that look like miniature pearls. Their round body shape shows they are not a hardy variety and should be kept indoors.

Moor

These goldfish are blackish in color. Their eyes often stick out more from their heads. They are then described as telescope-eyed.

The moor makes an interesting contrast to the usual bright colors of goldfish.

Fantail

This is another variety that is really only suited to an aquarium, where its graceful, flowing fins can be appreciated. The water must be kept very clean, otherwise the fins are likely to become ragged.

The bubble-eye needs to live in an aquarium without sharp rocks.

Bubble-eye

This has to be one of the weirdest of all goldfish varieties. The swellings under the eyes can be punctured quite easily, and so there should be no sharp rocks in a tank housing these goldfish.

Ryukin

This goldfish has a clear hump above the head, and the body is broad. The speckled pattern of this ryukin means that it is described as a calico.

The eyes of a goldfish are usually on the side of the head, as in this ryukin, but they may point upwards, towards the sky, such fish are called celestials.

Choosing your goldfish

You can buy goldfish from a number of places, including pet stores and aquatic outlets, which you can find in the yellow pages. If you want to see a number of different goldfish varieties, then you may be able to find a fish show in your area to visit, and there may be clubs that you can join as well. If you want to look for one of the rarer varieties, you may need to go to a breeder. There are various fish-keeping magazines that can help you to find such people.

Fancy fish are fun, but since they are bad swimmers, they are best suited to living in an aquarium.

Healthy fish

Look carefully at the fish before buying them. It is easier if they are in a tank so you can see them from the side, rather than a pool, where you look down on them from above. Healthy goldfish swim easily through the water. Beware of any of the fancy varieties that bob up and down in the water, since this is often a sign of a swim bladder problem, which is hard to cure. Look closely at their bodies, too, to check that there are no signs of injury. Beware of any strange bumps or damage to the fins although this can sometimes improve when the fish are housed in better surroundings.

Choose a safe, level base for your aquarium, at a height that you can watch the fish easily. Check that the tank will not be in direct sunlight.

Things to look for

If you are buying young goldfish, they may have dark areas on their bodies. These usually disappear as the fish grow older, so they will become more colorful, but in other cases, the colors of your fish should not change dramatically. You may want to choose several fish, particularly if you are going to keep them in a pond. It is very difficult, with young fish especially, to tell their sex reliably, but if you choose four, then hopefully, you should have at least one pair. Larger goldfish cost more than small ones, and they will also be older, which may make them harder to tame.

Goldfish are sociable and are happiest when they live with other goldfish, so you should buy more than one fish for your aquarium or pond.

Netting your goldfish

There are likely to be a number of goldfish in the tank, so be sure you can pick out your favorite from the aquarium easily. A special net will be used to scoop the fish out of the water. If you need to do this yourself, make sure that the fish cannot jump out by placing your hand over the top of the net.

Use a net to get your goldfish out of the water, and cover the top with your hand to stop it from escaping.

The final check

When the goldfish has been transferred to a clear plastic bag partly filled with water from the aquarium, check the fish again to be sure it is really healthy. Don't forget to look carefully at both sides of the body. Occasionally, a goldfish may hatch with only one eye. If you are happy with your choice, the seller will tie the bag up for you, usually adding extra oxygen first, and you can then take your goldfish home right away.

When it is in a clear bag, take one more look at your fish to make sure it has two eyes.

The home aquarium

It is always a good idea to set up the aquarium for your goldfish before you bring them home. This will give you the opportunity to check that everything is working properly. It also means that your fish can be transferred immediately to their new home, rather than having to stay in their traveling bag for longer than necessary. Setting up your tank will probably take about an hour.

The tank

Buy a large tank, even if you are choosing small fish, because this will give them plenty of space. A long tank is better than a round tank, because it gives the fish a bigger area for swimming. You can choose a tank that is made from glass or a clear plastic, called acrylic. This is lighter and easier to handle than glass, but it can also break if it is dropped.

Prepare your aquarium before you buy your fish. Put a filter underneath the gravel to help keep the water and the aquarium clean.

Fitting a filter

A filter will help to keep the aquarium clean. There are different types. One of the most common is an under-gravel filter. This fits directly over the entire floor of the aquarium, and the gravel is placed on top. The filter is connected to the air pump, which helps to move the water around the tank.

Gravel

There are many different types of gravel, but it is better to avoid bright-colored gravel that clashes with the color of your goldfish. If you want to keep moors, however, you may want to have white gravel to highlight their dark color.

Since it can be heavy, get an adult to help you put gravel in the aquarium.

Make sure you wash the gravel before putting it in the tank.

Filling the tank

Ordinary, fresh tap water contains chlorine compounds, which can kill fish. Therefore, you need to know how much water the tank holds, so you can add the right amount of a dechlorinator and water conditioner, to make the water safe for your goldfish. These water treatments can be bought from pet shops and large supermarkets.

When you are ready to fill the tank, put a clean saucer on top of the layer of gravel. Then slowly pour the treated water from a clean jug, pouring it carefully on the saucer to prevent the gravel from being stirred up.

Put a saucer on top of the gravel to prevent it from being stirred up as the dechlorinated water is added.

Plants in the aquarium

You can either choose plastic plants, which look like the real thing when they are in the aquarium, or cold water plants, which grow well in an unheated tank. Don't put too many plants in the aquarium, because this will make it hard for your goldfish to swim around. Try to position plants at the back of the tank, so you can still see the fish. Canadian pondweed is a popular choice for goldfish tanks.

Add rocks, plants, and ornaments to make your tank attractive to look at and homey for your fish.

A hood will not only stop your fish from jumping out, it will also stop the water from evaporating.

Hood and lighting

It is a good idea to have a hood to cover the aquarium. This will prevent the water from evaporating, and can include a light, which makes it easier to look at the fish. Don't leave the light on for more than eight hours a day, because microscopic plants in the water, called algae, will start growing on the glass, turning it green. Be very careful to keep water off the hood if it has a light, and don't touch the light without help from an adult.

Getting your goldfish settled

Getting your new fish home is exciting, but make sure you give it lots of time to settle into its new home.

It is really important to get everything ready for your goldfish ahead of time, and then allow your fish to settle down quietly in its new home. This means that it will be much less likely to get sick. Remember to add a water conditioner with a dechlorinator to the aquarium water first. This will help to heal any damage to the coat that protects the goldfish's body from infection. This coating can be easily damaged by handling, which is why you should never try to pick up your goldfish with your hands.

The early stages

When you bring your goldfish home, float the bag in the tank for about 20 minutes, so they will not get a shock from the change of temperature when you put them into the water. Then get someone to hold the bag open for you, so you can net the fish and move them into the aquarium, pouring the dirty water away. The fish are unlikely to want to eat immediately, but you can offer them some food later in the day. When they are settled, goldfish will usually need to be fed two or three times a day, although they can go without food for several days without coming to any harm.

When you put your goldfish into the tank, get some help and use a special net to put the fish into the water.

Food and feeding

A feeding ring that can be stuck to the inside of the tank can be useful if you are out a lot during the daytime.

Feeding habits

Goldfish instinctively look for food on the floor of the aquarium, which is why you often see them digging in the gravel, sometimes uprooting plants. But it is very easy to coax them into coming up and feeding at the surface of the water.

You can use a feeding ring to keep food in one place, making it easy to remove leftovers—the fish will soon learn where to look for their food. They may even take food from your fingers, but always wash your hands thoroughly, immediately after you feed them this way. An automatic feeder can be useful if you are out a lot during the day or if you are away on vacation.

Types of food

There are various specially prepared goldfish foods, which contain everything the fish need to stay healthy. Flake food is often given to young goldfish. It comes in fine wafers, which you can crumble up or drop on the water surface. Pellet foods for goldfish will also float, and these come in various sizes. Food sticks are also available, but these are only really suitable for large goldfish, usually those that live in ponds. There are special goldfish foods, such as growth foods, and others intended for certain varieties such as lionheads. Pond fish need special food that can be digested easily when the water temperature is low.

Different ages and breeds of goldfish like to eat different types of food.

Goldfish look for food in the gravel on the aquarium floor.

How much food?

The main mistake that many people make when feeding goldfish is to give them too much food. Leftover food can pollute the water in the tank, and may also make the fish sick. Don't give your fish any more food than they will eat in about five minutes, but feed them several times during the day, once they're settled down in their new surroundings.

Goldfish outdoors

A pond should be made in a sheltered site, but not in permanent shade. It is best to stay clear of deciduous trees, or you will have to use a net to keep fallen leaves out of the water. A level site will make it much easier to build the pond. Ponds can be made either by using a preformed shell buried in a hole, or by using a tough liner, which stops the water from sinking into the ground.

It is important to choose the right spot for the pond, so that your fish will be happy and safe.

young water lily

fully grown water lily

marginal shelf

Your pond should have more than one level. It should be deep in the middle and have a shallower area called a marginal shelf, so that you can grow different types of plants.

Ponds can be dangerous—wire mesh over the top will stop a child from falling in.

Preparing the pond

Dig the hole carefully and then check that the pond is level, using a tool called a level. If necessary, you can adjust the bedding material on which the pond will rest, or even remove more soil. Otherwise, it could end up looking a little like a sloping bathtub. What you want is to be able to hide all the edges of the pond, so that it looks natural. Most ponds have a projection around their edge below the water level which is known as the marginal shelf.

Water lilies and oxygenators

A favorite plant of many pond keepers is the water lily. There are many different types, so be sure to choose one that will not be too big for your pond. Water lilies grow fast in the spring, and their leaves spread over the surface of the pond, shading it and helping to prevent the water from becoming green.

Alongside the water lilies in the pond, add some oxygenating plants, like those grown in an aquarium. These oxygenators will spread rapidly, and although you will not see them clearly in a pond, they are vital for the fish— they give them somewhere to hide and breed.

Oxygenators may be hard to see in a pond, but they are very important because fish can hide and breed in them.

Avoiding freezing

Try to build the pond by late springtime, so the fish can acclimatize over the summer. If ice is likely in the winter, the pond must be at least 3 feet deep, so the fish will be safe away from the ice. You can get special pond heaters, which should keep part of the surface of the pond free from ice during the winter. Or floating a ball may help to prevent ice from forming. Do not smash the ice with a hammer, because vibrations can harm the fish. Instead, ask an adult to melt a hole using the base of a hot saucepan, but never try this yourself.

It may take a couple of years for water lilies to bloom, but their beautiful flowers are worth waiting for.

Baby pond fish

Goldfish that grow up in ponds can find natural food in the form of minute water creatures and plants. You may not even be aware that your goldfish have spawned (laid eggs) until you see their surviving young swimming around with them in the water. When the baby fish are tiny, they may be in danger from other pond-dwellers, including their own parents.

Regular care

One of the most important things you need to do to make sure that your fish stay healthy is to change about a quarter of the volume of the water in their aquarium every two or three weeks. You will need a bucket and a tank siphon, and then, with the help of an adult or a friend, you can use the siphon to take out some of the water. You won't usually have to catch the goldfish while you are cleaning their tank so they will not be disturbed.

Changing some of the water in the aquarium every two to three weeks will help keep your fish healthy.

Keeping the aquarium clean

Some siphons can be used to vacuum dirt out of the gravel as well as sucking out water, but try not to dislodge any aquarium plants at the same time. If there is a build-up of algae on the glass, you can wipe this off very easily, using either a specially designed, magnetic cleaner or a long-handled glass cleaner.

Refilling the tank

When you refill the tank, always add the dechlorinator and water conditioner to the fresh water first, so that this new water will be safe for your goldfish. Ideally, you should leave the water to stand overnight before pouring it into the aquarium. This is so that it warms up to room temperature, rather than using it directly from the cold water tap.

Wash your hands thoroughly after cleaning the tank, and always wear rubber gloves if you have cuts on your hands.

A long-handled glass cleaner makes cleaning the aquarium glass very easy.

Algal problems

If there is a lot of algae growing in the tank, it is usually because there is too much light. It could be that the light over the aquarium is being left on for too long each day. Switch off the light at an earlier time every day to see if this improves the situation. It might also be that the tank is exposed to bright sunlight. This can happen in the summer, when the sun's rays are stronger. Closing a curtain may help, or you may have to relocate the whole aquarium, with adult assistance. Adding a pond snail to the aquarium sometimes helps—snails eat the algae, although they may nibble the plants, too.

Vacation care

When you are going on vacation, goldfish present less of a problem than other pets. If you are away for just a short time, such as a weekend, you can provide them with a special food bar that dissolves slowly in the water without polluting it. If you are going away for longer, you can ask a friend or neighbor to take care of your fish, explaining how important it is not to overfeed them. Alternatively, you can buy an automatic feeder, which will feed your goldfish the required amount of food at set times.

Ask someone to feed your goldfish for you if you are going to be away for a long time.

Breeding goldfish

Female goldfish lay small, whitish eggs, releasing them from their bodies as part of a process known as spawning. Goldfish sometimes breed when they are just over a year old, but they usually do not produce many eggs when they are this young.

Male or female?

Goldfish normally spawn in the springtime and all through the summer, and it is usually possible to recognize the signs in advance. Females swell up with eggs, but male fish develop tiny white pimples on their gill covers, which you can see extending along the nearby fins. Soon, the male will be chasing the female around, and he will get very aggressive just before spawning occurs.

Save those eggs

Female goldfish may lay hundreds of eggs at a single spawning, but often only a small number of these eggs will survive long enough to hatch. This is because the adult fish do not recognize the eggs as their own, and so they will eat them as a snack. You should separate the goldfish from their eggs if they spawn.

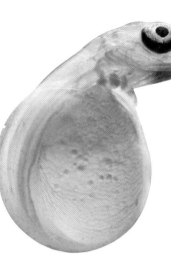

Newly hatched fry will not move much until they need more food.

If you want the eggs to hatch, you need to put them in another tank so they are not eaten.

Hatching

It will take several days for the eggs to hatch, depending on the water temperature. When they first emerge from the eggs, the young fish, which are called fry, just lie quietly. They are very tiny and have almost transparent bodies. When they have digested their yolk sacs, which you may locate as yellowish swellings under their bodies, the fry will start to swim around the tank looking for more food.

Caring for young goldfish

When they have just hatched, you will need to give baby fish a special food, and then, as they grow bigger, you can introduce them to flake food, which you must crush to powder by rubbing it with your fingers. Be sure to give the goldfish more space as they get bigger, to keep them from becoming overcrowded. You must also change the water frequently if they are in an aquarium.

Young fish need special food and lots of space so they can grow.

Fit and healthy

It is usually not difficult to tell when a goldfish is sick, because its behavior changes. The fish may be reluctant to swim, and will hang at an unusual angle in the water or gasp at the surface, not wanting to eat. Goldfish are most likely to get sick soon after you obtain them. Use a brand of fish food that contains vitamin C, and change the water regularly to help protect them against sickness.

It is easy to see when a fish is sick, so check them on a regular basis.

Parasites

Keep an eye on your goldfish for signs of parasites, such as white spot. The tiny, microscopic creatures that cause this illness spread through the water and then attack the goldfish's body, so that it looks like it is covered with white spots. Do not confuse this condition with the white pimples that allow you to recognize male goldfish—these do not cover the whole body. Special treatments for white spot can be bought in aquatic stores. Moving the goldfish to new surroundings on a temporary basis should also help, because the parasites in the water will die within in a few days if they cannot find a host.

Poisoning

Everyday household aerosols, such as polish and air fresheners, can be deadly to goldfish, so don't use them anywhere near the tank. Even outside, spraying your cat or dog for fleas, or using weed killers and pesticides, can be fatal if any spray blows onto the surface of the pond, so always be careful.

Fungus

Fungal infections often follow an injury to the goldfish's body. Fungus looks a bit like cotton, and it can spread quickly if it is left untreated. Your pet is more likely to recover fully if treatment is started without delay. Always be sure that you make up the medication to the correct strength.

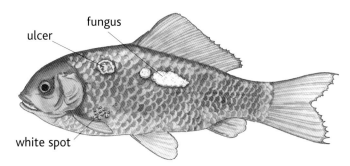

fungus

ulcer

white spot

White spots like these on the body of your goldfish may be a sign that your fish has parasites and that it needs to be moved or treated immediately.

This edition is published by Lorenz Books

Lorenz Books is an imprint of Anness Publishing Ltd
Hermes House, 88–89 Blackfriars Road, London SE1 8HA
tel. 020 7401 2077; fax 020 7633 9499
www.lorenzbooks.com; info@anness.com

© Anness Publishing Ltd 2003

This edition distributed in the U.K. by The Manning Partnership Ltd, 6 The Old Dairy, Melcombe Road,
Bath BA2 3LR; tel. 01225 478 444; fax 01225 478 440; sales@manning-partnership.co.uk

This edition distributed in the USA and Canada by National Book Network, 4501 Forbes Boulevard, Suite 200,
Lanham, MD 20706; tel. 301 459 3366; fax 301 429 5746; www.nbnbooks.com

This edition distributed in Australia by Pan Macmillan Australia, Level 18, St Martins Tower, 31 Market St,
Sydney, NSW 2000; tel. 1300 135 113; fax 1300 135 103; customer.service@macmillan.com.au

This edition distributed in New Zealand by David Bateman Ltd, 30 Tarndale Grove, Off Bush Road,
Albany, Auckland; tel. (09) 415 7664; fax (09) 415 8892

A CIP catalogue record for this book is available from the British Library.

Publisher: Joanna Lorenz
Managing Editor: Linda Fraser
Editor: Sarah Uttridge
Editorial Reader: Penelope Goodare
Production Controller: Darren Price
Designer: Linda Penny
Photographer: Paul Bricknell

The publishers would like to thank Hannah Lie, Conor Maguire, Liam Maguire,
and Jake Martin for modeling for this book.
Picture credits: David Alderton: 2br, 15tl, 15r, 15bl; Corbis: 18t, 18bl

1 3 5 7 9 10 8 6 4 2